# AMAZING ANIMALS

# Ocean Odyssey

First published 2010 by Macmillan Children's Books
a division of Macmillan Publishers Limited
20 New Wharf Road, London N1 9RR
Basingstoke and Oxford
Associated companies throughout the world
www.panmacmillan.com

ISBN: 978-0-230-74380-9 (HB)
ISBN: 978-0-330-51011-0 (PB)

Text copyright © Tony Mitton 2010
Illustrations copyright © Ant Parker 2010
Moral rights asserted.
Consultancy by David Burnie

1 3 5 7 9 8 6 4 2

A CIP catalogue record for this book is available from the British Library.

Printed in China

To Esmé Lucia Constance McCrum
from Tony Mitton, with best fishes
For Matt and Freddy - Ant

# AMAZING ANIMALS

# Ocean Odyssey

# Tony Mitton and Ant Parker

MACMILLAN CHILDREN'S BOOKS

The North Pacific Ocean
is vast and dark and deep.

It's home to many creatures
that swim and float and creep.

Here's a giant octopus.
Before you chase it, think!

It squirts whatever worries it
with brown and cloudy ink.

Basking sharks just drift along.
That's the way they feed.

Small creatures glide into their mouths
to give them what they need.

A jellyfish swims gently.
It seems to sway and swish.

Its stinging tentacles are used
for stunning little fish.

Angler fish are awesome.
They dangle bait that's bright.

When prey swims up to check it out,
they wait . . . and then they bite!

A giant squid looks scary.
It stares with googly eyes.

To meet a giant squid can give you
quite a big surprise!

When you're near a marlin,
remember to watch out.

It's sometimes called a spearfish
because of that sharp snout.

Sea otters dive for shellfish
from kelp beds near the shore.

They tuck them in a flap of skin,
and make a little store.

Dolphins are such friendly creatures.
Meet them in the bay.

They'll come and swim beside your boat
and leap around and play.

We've drifted round the ocean
to find what there might be.

But were you looking carefully?
What else did you see?

# Did you see . . .

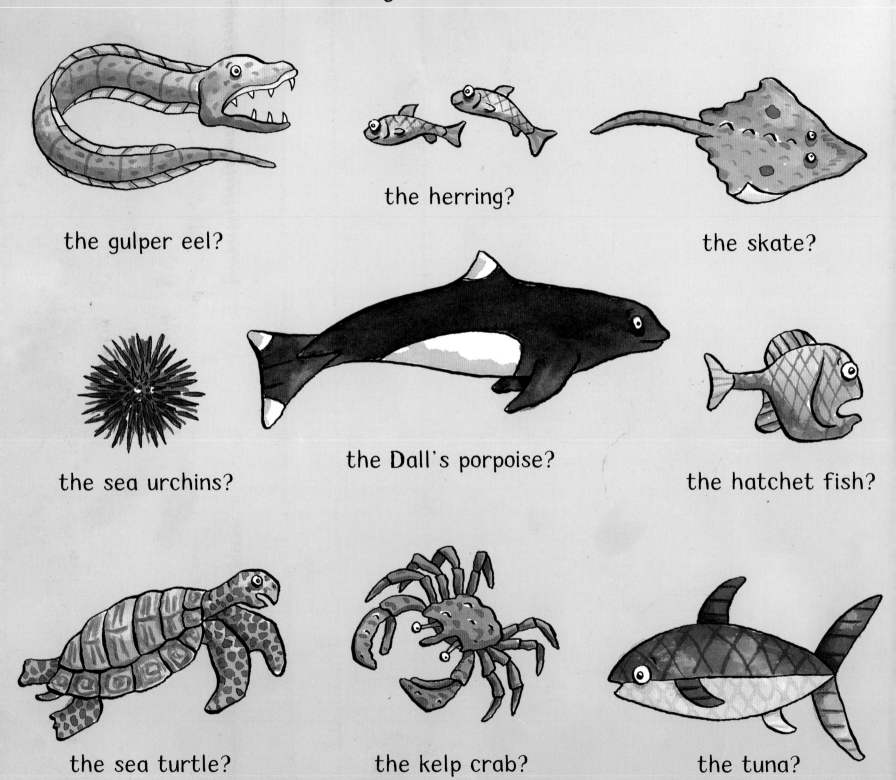

the gulper eel?

the herring?

the skate?

the sea urchins?

the Dall's porpoise?

the hatchet fish?

the sea turtle?

the kelp crab?

the tuna?